TEAM Together

T0351606

Top Tips and Practice
for PTE Young Learners

FIRSTWORDS & SPRINGBOARD

Contents

Introduction

Hello!

This book will help you to prepare for the PTE Young Learners *Firstwords* and *Springboard* tests.

The first part of this book will help you prepare for the tests, and includes:

- useful grammar tips, topics and words for *Firstwords* and *Springboard*
- general exam tips
- pronunciation and alphabet tips
- activities and tips in the *Strategies and Exercises* section.

The second part of the book has two past papers for you to complete, one for *Firstwords* and one for *Springboard*. Try to complete each paper in one attempt. If you get a good score, you'll be ready for the actual test!

The *Firstwords* written test is divided into six tasks:

- Tasks One and Two test your listening skills
- Tasks Three, Four and Five test your reading skills
- Task Six tests your writing skills.

The *Firstwords* spoken test is divided into two tasks:

- Task One has a conversation based on a board game
- Task Two has short talks based on topic cards, such as *my friends*, *my bedroom* and *my toys*.

The *Springboard* written test is divided into six tasks:

- Tasks One and Two test your listening skills
- Tasks Three and Four test your reading skills
- Tasks Five and Six test your writing skills.

The *Springboard* spoken test is divided into two tasks:

- Task One has a conversation based on a board game
- Task Two has short talks based on topic cards, such as *my family*, *at the weekend* and *my day at school*.

The audio scripts and answer keys for this book can be found online.

General exam tips

Before the test

- Review the test structure.

- Look back through your English notebook and review the important things.

- Check the word list in your book (see pages 8 and 9): do you remember all the words?

- Review the grammar points in your book (see pages 8 and 9).

- Be ready with pencils, a sharpener, an eraser and your ID document.

- Go to the bathroom!

During the test

- Listen carefully to the examiner.

- Read the instructions on the test paper.

- If you do not understand what you have to do, raise your hand.

- Write the answers clearly.

- Check the answers: you can always erase and rewrite!

- Do not talk to others.

After the test

- Submit your test paper (First, check that you have written your name!).

- Collect all your things.

- Leave the classroom silently.

- Relax!

- Your test results will arrive by mail.

Good luck!

Pronunciation

In English there are 5 vowels:

A E I O U

But there are 20 different sounds to pronounce them!

A

cat

car

train

chair

E

tree

computer

egg

ear

I

fish

bike

bird

O

clock

horse

boot

phone

owl

boy

tourist

U

bull

up

The alphabet

1. Look at the alphabet.

(A) B C D E F G H I (J) (K) L M
N O P Q R S T U V W X Y Z

2. Circle the letters that have the same sound in the same colour; the first one has been done for you.

3. Match the letters to the correct picture.

J K W X Y

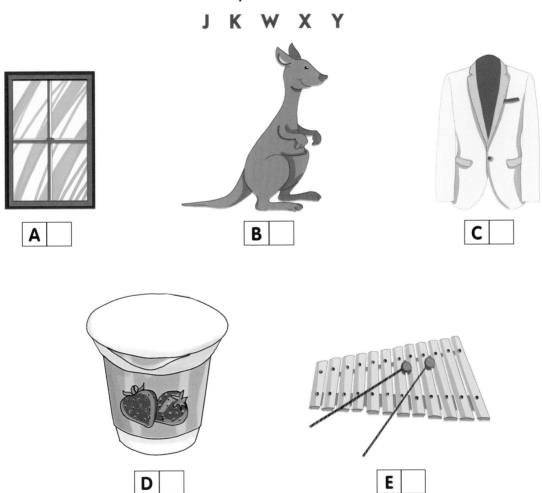

A ☐   B ☐   C ☐

D ☐   E ☐

For the *Firstwords* test, you need to know ...

... these grammar points:

- **'Has / Have got'**
  I've got a dog. Has he got a dog?
  He hasn't got a cat.
- **'There is / There are'**
  How many dogs are there?
- **The imperative and negative imperative**
  Get up! Sit down! Be quiet! Don't touch!
- **The verb 'to be' in the present tense**
  He's John. Are you Mary? I'm not tired.
- **The present continuous**
  Mr Brown is watching television.
- **'Can' for ability and requests**
  Mrs Brown can swim.
- **'Let's' for simple suggestions**
  Let's go to the cinema.
- **Basic question words**
  What?
  Where?
  What colour?
  Who?
  How many?
  How much?
  Which?
- **Demonstratives – pronouns and adjectives**
  This is, That's, Is this/that? This book is good.
- **Possessive 's'**
  Ben's book
- **Personal and possessive pronouns and adjectives**
  I, mine, my, ...
- **Plural of nouns**
  books, cats, classes, houses, children, men, women
- **Prepositions of place**
  The book is on/under/by the chair.
- **Simple conjunctions**
  and, but

... these topics:

- Hobbies
- Families
- Pets and animals
- School
- The body and people's appearance
- Toys
- Houses
- Common Places (park, cinema, ...)

... and these words:

- **Simple colours**
  red, blue, green, yellow
- **Nouns for family members**
  mother, father, Mum, Dad, brother, sister, aunt, uncle, grandma, grandad
- **Numbers from 1 to 20**
- **The house**
  kitchen, bathroom, bedroom, garden
- **Parts of the body**
  arm, leg, head, back
- **Children's clothes**
  T-shirt, shorts, sweatshirt, baseball cap, trainers
- **Basic adjectives for feelings**
  happy, sad, tired, hungry
- **Common pets and wild animals**
  dog, cat, tortoise, hamster, snake, monkey, lion, tiger
- **Common toys/playthings**
  bicycle, computer games, doll
- **Verbs often used for classroom instruction**
  sit down, stand up, open your books, write, fill in
- **Classroom objects**
  book, pencil, pen, ruler, school bag

For the *Springboard* test, you need to know …

… these grammar points:

- The present continuous – interrogative and negative
  Is Ben wearing a red T-shirt?
  Annie isn't eating a cheeseburger.
- 'Like' (or 'love') + '…ing'
  Ben doesn't like getting up early.
  Sophie loves school.
- The simple present for habits – affirmative, interrogative and negative
  Lions eat meat.
  The baby doesn't eat chips.
  Does Mrs Brown start work at 8.00?
- Adverbs of frequency
  sometimes, always, never, often
- Other question words
  How often?
  What kind?
  What time?
  How much?
- Verb + infinitive
  want to, help to, plan to, decide to
- Simple ordinals
  first, second, third
- Conjunctions
  when, before, after + *then* (adverb)
- Prepositions
  opposite, between, in front of

… these topics:

- Clothes
- Food
- Description of animals
- Homes

… and these words:

- Days of the week
  Monday, Tuesday, Wednesday
- Months of the year
  March, April, May
- Seasons and weather
  winter, spring, rain, sunshine
- Clothes and accessories
  coat, jacket, trainers, sweatshirt, T-shirt, scarf, …
- Words associated with clothes
  button, zip, laces
- Food and drink
  eggs, meat, bread, apple, cabbage, rice, water, juice, ….
- Fast food
  hamburgers, milkshake, chips, …
- Continents
  Europe, Asia, …
- Wild animals
  camel, crocodile, giraffe, hippo, rhino, …
- Basic words to describe the appearance of animals
  stripes, spots, feathers, wings, shell
- Rooms in a house or flat
  bedroom, bathroom, kitchen, living room
- Parts of a house or flat
  door, window, floor, wall, …
- Furniture and household objects
  bed, table, lamp, carpet, telephone, washing machine
- Sports children play and/or watch
  football, tennis, gymnastics

> **Remember: for the *Springboard* exam, you also need to know the grammar, topics and words required for the *Firstwords* exam.**

Activities for *Firstwords* Task 1

The *Listening* exercises can be difficult. Ask your teacher or parent to help you.

Remember:

- Read the instructions carefully.
- Listen to the audio twice.
- Listen for information you need to complete the exercise.
- Check your answers.

TOP TIPS

First, look at the pictures.

- What do you see in the pictures?
- Who do you see?
- What is happening?

Do Exercises 1, 2, 3 and 4 on page 11.

Do you need to review the grammar?

Review

- the *present simple*
- the *present continuous.*

Think about these topics:

- *houses*
- *hobbies.*

☞ In Exercise 2, the question is:
What is Olivia doing?

In **recording** 🎧 2 (page 44), you will hear Olivia and her mum talk about four activities.

Remember: you have to say what Olivia is doing *now*.

- *Come* and *play* are *present simple.* ✗
- *I'm not playing* is *present continuous*, but in the negative form. ✗
- *I'm sending an email* is *present continuous*, in the affirmative form. ✔

☞ In Exercise 3, the question is:
Where is Olivia?

In **recording** 🎧 3 (page 44), Nick and Olivia talk about four places.

Remember: say where Olivia is *now*.

- Mum is *outside*. ✗
- Lunch will be in the *garden* later, not now. ✗
- Olivia has to go to the *kitchen*. She is not there now. ✗
- Olivia is on the sofa in the *living room*. ✔

1. Look at the pictures. What is Olivia doing in each picture? Write A, B, C or D next to each sentence (1–4).

1. ☐ Olivia is reading a book. **3.** ☐ Olivia is sending an email.

2. ☐ Olivia is watching TV. **4.** ☐ Olivia is listening to music.

2. Now listen to recording 🎧2. What is Olivia doing? Tick the correct picture (A–D) in Exercise 1.

3. Listen to recording 🎧3. Where is Olivia? Tick the correct picture (A–D).

4. Complete this sentence:

Olivia is _____ on her tablet on the _____ .

Let's do some more *Listening* exercises!

Do Exercises 1, 2 and 3 on page 13.

Do you need to review the grammar?

Review

- words to ask questions (*what, where, who, ...*)
- *let's* to make suggestions.

Think about these topics:

- *common places*
- *family.*

☞ In Exercise 2, the question is:
Where does Nick want to go?

In **recording** 🎧4🎧 (page 44), Nick and Olivia talk about three places.

Remember: you have to say where Nick wants to go, *not* Olivia.

- Olivia wants to go to the *cinema*. ✗
- Nick wants to go to the *park*. ✔
- Olivia wants to *stay home*. ✗

☞ In Exercise 3, the questions are:
1. *Where do Nick and Olivia agree to go?*

In **recording** 🎧5🎧 (page 44), Nick and Olivia talk about *where* to go on a day out.

Remember: you have to say the place where both Nick and Olivia agree to go.

- Nick wants to go to the *park*, but Olivia says no. ✗
- Olivia wants to go to the *cinema*. ✗
- Olivia wants to go to the *museum*, and Nick says yes. ✔

2. *When do they want to go?*

In **recording** 🎧5🎧 (page 44), Nick and Olivia talk about *when* to go on their day out.

Remember: you have to say the day when Nick and Olivia want to go to the museum.

- Mum wants to go today, but Nick says no. ✗
- Nick wants to go tomorrow, and Olivia says yes. ✔

3. *Who do they want to go with?*

In **recording** 🎧5🎧 (page 44), Nick and Olivia talk about *who* they want to go with on their day out.

Remember: you have to say who Nick and Olivia want to go with.

- Grandma and Grandad. ✔
- Hamish, the dog. ✗
- Mum and Dad. ✔

1. Look at the pictures. Where are Nick and Olivia in each picture? Write A, B, C or D next to each sentence.

A

B

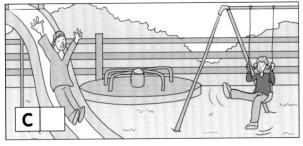

C

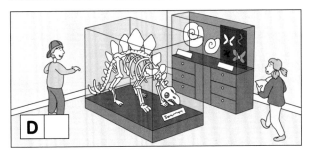

D

1. ☐ Nick and Olivia are at the park.

2. ☐ Nick and Olivia are at home.

3. ☐ Nick and Olivia are at the museum.

4. ☐ Nick and Olivia are at the cinema.

2. Now listen to recording 🎧4. Where does Nick want to go? Tick the correct picture (A–D) in Exercise 1.

3. Listen to recording 🎧5. Tick the correct picture, A, B or C.

1. Where do Nick and Olivia agree to go?

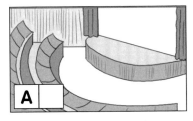

A

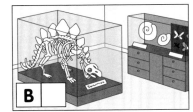

B

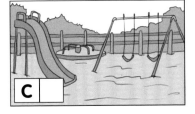

C

2. When do they want to go?

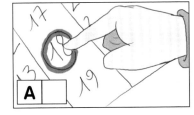

A

B

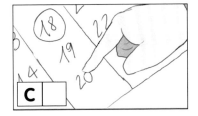

C

3. Who do they want to go with?

A

B

C

Activities for *Firstwords* Task 2

The *Listening* exercises can be difficult. Ask your teacher or parent to help you.

Remember:

- Read the instructions carefully.
- Listen to the audio twice.
- Listen for information you need to complete the exercise.
- Check your answers.

TOP TIPS

First, look at the pictures.

- Who is in the picture?
- What are people doing in the picture?

Do Exercises 1, 2, 3 and 4 on page 15.

Do you need to review the grammar?

Review

- the verb *to be*.
- the verb *have / has got*.

Think about this topic:

- adjectives to describe people.

☞ In Exercise 2, the question is:
Who is Nick talking to?

Listen to **recording 🎧6🎧** (page 44). *Who is Nick talking to now?*

- Nick is Olivia's brother. You need the name of his friend. ✗
- Tom is tall and thin. Nick is talking to a short and thin friend. ✗
- Mike is short and thin. He has blond hair. The father says the boy is tall, thin and has dark hair. ✗
- Justin has dark hair, but he is short. He's got glasses. ✗
- Olivia sees her brother, Nick, talking to a tall and thin friend with short, dark hair. He is Phil. ✔

☞ In Exercise 3, the question is:
Write the names of Nick's friends under the pictures in Exercise 1.

Remember: you have the descriptions from Exercise 1.

The information in **recording 🎧7🎧** (page 44) helps you:

- Justin is the only boy with glasses. This is easy! Write **Justin** under picture **D**.
- Phil is tall and has brown hair. Write **Phil** under picture **A**.
- Mike and Justin are both short, but Mike does not have glasses. Write **Mike** under picture **C**.
- Tom is tall with black hair. Write **Tom** under picture **B**.

1. Look at the pictures. Who is Nick talking to in each picture? Match each picture (A–D) to the correct sentence (1–4). Draw lines.

A

_____

C

_____

1. Nick is talking to a tall boy with short, brown hair.

2. Nick is talking to a short boy.

3. Nick is talking to a short boy with glasses.

4. Nick is talking to a tall boy.

B

_____

D

_____

2. Now listen to recording ▸6◂ . Who is Nick talking to? Write A, B, C or D here:

_____

3. Listen to recording ▸7◂ . Write the names of Nick's friends under the pictures in Exercise 1.

4. Complete these sentences.

   1. Nick is with _____ at the park. Phil is _____ .
      He has got _____ .

   2. Then Nick helps _____ to find his glasses.

Let's do some more *Listening* exercises!

Do Exercises 1, 2 and 3 on page 17.

Do you need to review the grammar?

Review

- the verb *to be*
- the verb *have / has got*
- prepositions of place (*on, over, ...*).

Think about these topics:

- *adjectives to describe people*
- *clothes*
- *hobbies.*

☞ **In Exercise 2, the question is:**

Who is Olivia practising with?

In **recording** 🎧 8 (page 45), Nick talks about who Olivia is practising with.

Remember: you have to say *who* Olivia is practising with, *not* who is on stage.

- There are two girls with flowers in their hair, but Olivia is practising with only one girl. ✘
- Olivia is not dancing with the girl who has flowers in her hair and is wearing black trousers. ✘
- Olivia is next to the girl with flowers in her hair and is wearing a long dress. ✔

☞ **In Exercise 3, draw lines to match names and pictures.**

In **recording** 🎧 9 (page 45), Nick, Mum and Dad talk about Olivia and her friends.

Remember: there are two extra pictures.

- Annabelle is wearing trousers and a T-shirt. She has short hair. ✔
- Sophie has a long dress and has short hair. ✔
- Viola has a skirt and flowers in her hair. ✘
- Martin wears a hat and shorts. ✔
- Linda has a teddy bear. ✔
- Asia has a dress and has flowers in her hair. ✘

1. Look at the pictures. Who is Olivia with in each picture? Match each picture (A–D) to the correct sentence (1–4). Draw lines.

1. Olivia is with a girl who is wearing flowers in her hair.

2. Olivia is with a girl who is wearing a long dress.

3. Olivia is with a girl who has short hair and is wearing dark trousers.

4. Olivia is with a girl who is wearing a dress and flowers in her hair.

2. Now listen to recording ⟨8⟩. Who is Olivia practising with? Write A, B, C or D here:

3. Listen to recording ⟨9⟩. Draw a line from the names (1–6) to the pictures (A–H) of Olivia's ballet friends. Be careful. There are two extra pictures.

1. Annabelle
2. Sophie
3. Viola
4. Martin
5. Linda
6. Asia

Activities for *Firstwords* Task 3

It helps to know lots of words and topics to do these *Reading* and *Matching* exercises. Ask your teacher or parent to help you.

Remember:

- Read the instructions carefully.
- Look for similar words in questions and answers.
- Check your answers.

TOP TIPS

First, read the sentences.

- What kind of questions are they? Do you answer with *yes* or *no*? These are closed questions. Does the answer give information or express an opinion? This is an open question. The answer to a *Wh*-question is never *yes* or *no*.
- Read the questions. Look for the answer that contains similar words.
- Check again. Then match a question to an answer.

Do Exercises 1, 2, 3 and 4 on page 19.

Do you need to review the grammar?

Review

- words to ask questions (*what, where, who, ...*)
- the verb *can* to make suggestions or requests.

Think about these topics:

- *families*
- *common places.*

☞ **In Exercise 2, choose the correct answer (A or B) for each question.**

In **recording** 🎧10 (page 45), you will hear key words: you do not need to guess.

☞ **In Exercise 3, match Nick's questions (A–D) to Mum's answers (1–4).**

In **recording** 🎧11 (page 45), Nick talks to his mum about organising a party.

Remember: underline similar words.

A   Can we have a party for Grandma next week?

B   Can we have the party at the <u>swimming pool</u>?

C   Can we have the party at the <u>cinema</u>?

D   Can we have the party at the <u>park</u>?

1.   No, Nick! Grandma doesn't like watching <u>films</u>.

2.   Yes, Grandma loves going to the <u>park</u> to see the ducks.

3.   Yes, that would be good, Nick.

4.   No, Nick! Grandma doesn't like <u>swimming</u>.

Question **A** is a closed question, with a simple answer (3. *Yes, ...*).

The other questions have words that go together with words in the answer.

1. Match the questions (1–3) to the answers (A–C). Draw lines.

1.	Who is that?	**A**	Doris.
2.	What's her name?	**B**	Near the park.
3.	Where does she live?	**C**	My grandma.

2. Now listen to recording 🎧 **10** . Tick the correct answer (A or B) for each question (1–3).

1. When is Grandma's birthday?   **A** ☐ This week.   **B** ☐ Next week.

2. What is Olivia going to do?   **A** ☐ Buy a present.   **B** ☐ Make a cake.

3. Who is going to buy Grandma a present?   **A** ☐ Nick.   **B** ☐ Olivia.

3. Listen to recording 🎧 **11** . Match Nick's questions (1–4) to Mum's answers (A–D). Draw lines.

1. Can we have a birthday party for Grandma next week?

A No, Nick! Grandma doesn't like watching films.

2. Can we have the party at the swimming pool?

B Oh yes, Grandma loves going to the park to see the ducks.

3. Can we have the party at the cinema?

C Yes, that would be good, Nick.

4. Can we have the party at the park?

D No, Nick! Grandma doesn't like swimming.

4. Answer these questions.

1. Can Nick have a birthday party for Grandma?

_____

2. Can they have the birthday party at the swimming pool or cinema?

_____

3. Where is the party?

_____

4. When do they want to have the party?

_____

Activities for *Firstwords* Task 4

It helps to know lots of words and topics to do these *Reading* and *Matching* exercises. Ask your teacher or parent to help you.

Remember:

- Read the instructions carefully.
- Look for words that describe things or actions you see in the pictures.
- Check your answers.

TOP TIPS

First, look at the pictures.

- What do you see in the picture?
- Who do you see?
- What is happening?

Do Exercises 1, 2, 3 and 4 on page 21.

Do you need to review the grammar?

Review

- demonstrative adjectives (*this window, that cat, those cats*)
- the imperative (**Look** *at that cat!*)
- words to ask questions (*have, who, what*).

Think about these topics:

- *pets*
- *family*
- *houses*
- *appearance.*

☞ In Exercise 1, match the topics to the correct questions.

Remember: you have to look for words that go with the topic in the sentences.

☞ In Exercise 2, match the pictures to the correct sentence.

Remember: you have to look for the sentence that matches the people, things or actions in the picture.

- In **picture 1**, Nick is not checking the size of the window ✘. He is opening the window. ✔
- In **picture 2**, Nick does not want Lucy's pen ✘. They are looking for the pen. ✔

- In **picture 3**, there are two cats. *That* is singular ✘. *Those* is plural. ✔
- In **picture 4**, James is playing tennis ✔. We do not know if he likes it. ✘

☞ In Exercise 3, match the picture to the correct sentence.

Remember: you have to look for the sentence that matches the people, things or actions in the picture.

- 1 Olivia needs to give her name to join the school.
- 2 The dance teacher asks Olivia and her friends to stop talking.
- 3 Olivia goes to meet her dance teacher.
- 4 Those are not Olivia's shoes.

1. Match the topics (1–4) to the correct question (A or B). Draw lines.

| 1. PETS | **A** Have you got a dog? |
| | **B** Do you like tigers? |

| 3. HOME | **A** Where is your school? |
| | **B** Where do you live? |

| 2. FAMILY | **A** Who is your best friend? |
| | **B** What is your sister's name? |

| 4. APPEARANCE | **A** What colour is your hair? |
| | **B** What's your favourite colour? |

2. Match the pictures (1–4) to the correct sentence (A or B). Draw lines.

A Let's open this window, it's hot.

B This window is very big.

A I like your red pen, Lucy.

B Your pen is under the table, Lucy.

A Look at that cat.

B Look at those cats.

A James is over there. He's playing tennis.

B James likes playing tennis.

3. Look at the pictures of Olivia's first day at her new dance school. Match each picture (1–4) to the correct sentence (A–D).

A This is your teacher, Mrs Jackson.

B Are these your ballet shoes?

C What is your name?

D Stop talking, please, children.

4. Write the questions / sentences from Exercise 3, in the correct order, here:

1. ☐ 2. ☐ 3. ☐ 4. ☐

Activities for *Firstwords* Task 5

It helps to know lots of words and topics to do these *Reading* and *Matching* exercises. Ask your teacher or parent to help you.

Remember:

- Read the instructions carefully.
- Check your answers.

TOP TIPS

First, look at the pictures.

- What do you see in the picture?
- Do you see a person, an animal or a thing?

Do Exercises 1, 2, 3 and 4 on page 23.

Think about these topics:

- *toys*
- *people's appearance*
- *school*
- *animals.*

☞ In Exercise 1, match the topics to the correct word lists.

- Topic 1 is *toys*.
- Topic 2 is *clothes*.
- Topic 3 is *school*.
- Topic 4 is *animals*.

Remember: there is one extra word list.

- List C contains the names of rooms.

There are bathrooms in schools, but there are no bedrooms! ✘

The rooms in the list are rooms in a house. *Houses* is not a topic. ✔

☞ In Exercise 2, add two words to each list.

- Use a dictionary to help you.

☞ In Exercise 3, match pictures to the words.

Remember: you have to match each word to one picture.

- Check which words are singular (*computer, desk, window*) and which words are plural (*elephants, books, hats*). There are three words that are singular and three words that are plural.

- Look for pictures that show only one object and pictures that show more than one.

- Match singular words (2, 3 and 5) with pictures that have only one object (B, C, F).

- Match plural words (1, 4 and 6) with pictures that have more than one object (A, D, E).

1. Match each word list (A–D) to each topic box (1–4). Draw lines. Be careful – there is one extra word list.

A   sweatshirt, baseball hat, trainers

B   book, pencil, ruler

C   kitchen, bedroom, bathroom

D   monkey, lion, tiger

E   bike, computer game, doll

| 1. TOYS |
| 2. CLOTHES |
| 3. SCHOOL |
| 4. ANIMALS |

2. Add two more words to each topic (1–4). Use the words in the box below to help you.

> pen • hippopotamus • giraffe • T-shirt
> board • ball • shorts • bike

1.   TOYS   _____

2.   CLOTHES   _____

3.   SCHOOL   _____

4.   ANIMALS   _____

3. Olivia goes to visit her new friend from the dance school. Her new friend is called Viola. Olivia sees many things in Viola's bedroom. Match the pictures (A–F) to the words (1–6). Draw lines.

1.   elephants

2.   computer

3.   desk

4.   books

5.   window

6.   hats

4. Complete the sentences. Use the words from Exercise 3.

Viola has got many things in her bedroom. She has got a _____ , a _____ and many _____ . She has also got a _____ .

Activities for *Firstwords* Task 6

It helps to know lots of words and topics to do these *Reading* and *Matching* exercises. Ask your teacher or parent to help you.

Remember:

- Read the instructions carefully.
- Think about what kind of word you need to complete each space (verbs, nouns, adjectives, ...).
- There are three extra words.
- Check your answers.

TOP TIPS

First, read the text and the words in the box.

- What is the text about?
- Which words in the box can you use to complete the sentences?
- Do you need a noun (for example, *dog*, *house*), a verb (*is*, *am*), an adjective (*big*, *tall*), a pronoun (*I*, *she*) ...?
- Which words in the box are extra?

Do Exercises 1, 2, 3 and 4 on page 25.

Do you need to review the grammar?

Review

- personal pronouns (*I, you, he, she, ...*)
- the verb *to be* and the verb *can*
- the order of words in a sentence
- *adjectives*.

☞ In Exercise 1, write each word in the correct box.

Remember: think about what kind of words you have.

- Does this word describe people or things? If yes, it is an adjective.
- Does this word indicate *who* does the action or *who* is speaking? If yes, it is a personal pronoun.
- Is the word the name of an animal, a thing or a person? If yes, it is a noun.
- Does this word describe *what* or *how* an object or a person is? If so, it is the verb *to be*.

☞ In Exercise 2, put the words in the correct order to form a sentence.

Remember: always start with the subject, and put the adjectives before the names.

☞ In Exercise 3, write the missing words.

Remember: you have to make sure the grammar is correct.

- What is the text about?
- Which words come before and after the space?
- What information do you need to complete the sentence? For example, a personal pronoun is needed for gap 1 and an adjective is needed for gap 2.

1. Write each word (1–8) in the correct box (A–D).

1. am
2. happy
3. ballet shoes
4. is
5. I
6. house
7. she
8. big

A NOUNS

_____

_____

B VERB 'TO BE'

_____

_____

C ADJECTIVES

_____

_____

D PERSONAL PRONOUNS

_____

_____

2. Put the words in the correct order.

☐ BOY   ☐ IS   ☐ A   ☐ HAPPY   ☐ HE

3. Olivia writes in her diary about her new friend, Viola. Write the missing words to help her finish. Use the words in the box. Be careful – there are three extra words.

> big • I • is • dog • she • horrible
> can • house • am • tall

(1) _____ have got a new friend. Her name is Viola. She is (2) _____

and she (3) _____ always happy. We go to dance class together on

Saturdays.

Viola (4) _____ dance very well. Her (5) _____ is near where I live.

She has got a (6) _____ dog. I like dogs. Her (7) _____ is very nice.

4. Complete the sentences about YOUR friend.

My friend _____ . _____ in order to write My friend

_____ . [Her] name is _____ .

He/She is _____ and _____ .

Activities for *Firstwords Speaking* Task 7

The *Speaking* exercises can be difficult. Ask your teacher or parent to help you.

Remember:

- Listen carefully to the examiner's instructions.
- Always ask and answer questions in sentences.
- Show the examiner that you know the grammar and vocabulary.
- Ask the examiner if you do not understand something.

TOP TIPS

First, look at the questions and pictures on the squares from the board game carefully.

- What do you see in the picture?
- Can you correctly pronounce the question on the card?
- How can you answer?

Remember: count out loud in English as you move from square to square on the game!

Do Exercises 1, 2, 3 and 4 on page 27.

Do you need to review the grammar and vocabulary?

See the topics list on page 8. Which topics do you need to study more?

☞ **In Exercise 2, answer the questions.**

Remember: questions that start with *Wh-* (*Who, What, Where, ...*) are open questions. They give information or an opinion.

Questions that start with *Have you ...? Can you ...?* (or *Are you ...?*) are closed questions. The answers need to start with *Yes* or *No*. Then, you can add more information.

- **Question 1:** here you can only give one answer!
- **Question 2:** say the name of the food.

If you cannot remember the name of your favourite food, say another one you can remember! The examiner does not know what you like!

- **Questions 3–6:** you can reply *Yes* or *No*, and add information. For example, if you have sisters or siblings, or the name of your own *pet*, ...

☞ **In Exercise 3, answer the questions.**

Remember: try to pronounce the words correctly. For example, if you have to say something in the plural, say the 's' at the end of the word clearly.

- **Question A:** be careful about the English pronunciation of vowels.
- **Question B:** the answer is a number.
- **Question C:** the answer is a colour.
- **Question D:** the answer is the name of your city and country.

1. Match the sentence halves (1–6) and (A–F).

1.	What is your first name?	**A**	It's ice-cream.
2.	What is your favourite food?	**B**	Yes, I've got a dog.
3.	Have you got a big family?	**C**	No, I can't.
4.	Have you got a pet?	**D**	It's Henry.
5.	Can you speak Spanish?	**E**	Yes, I can. Hola!
6.	Can you sing?	**F**	No, I'm an only child.

2. Ask the questions in Exercise 1 to a classmate.

3. Look at these squares from a board game. Work with a partner. Ask and answer the questions.

A

Can you spell your name?

B

How many books have you got
in your school bag?

C

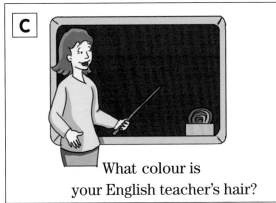

What colour is
your English teacher's hair?

D

Where do you live?

4. Write three more questions that Olivia can ask Mr Duffy. Invent the answers.

Questions   **Answers**

1. _____   _____

2. _____   _____

3. _____   _____

Activities for *Firstwords Speaking* Task 8

The *Speaking* exercises can be difficult. Ask your teacher or parent to help you.

Remember:

- Listen carefully to the examiner's instructions.
- Show the examiner that you know the grammar and vocabulary.
- Ask the examiner if you do not understand something.

TOP TIPS

First, look at the picture on the topic card and read the topic carefully.

- What do you see in the picture?
- What do you need to talk about?
- What grammar and vocabulary do you need to talk about it?

Remember: you have to pay attention to the pronunciation!

Do Exercises 1, 2, 3 and 4 on page 29.

Do you need to review the grammar and vocabulary?

Review

- see the list on page 8 – which topics do you need to study more?

☞ **In Exercise 3, you will talk about these topics:**

A   Animals
B   My house
C   Food
D   My hobbies

Remember: you have to speak for one minute. Do not go too fast. Speak slowly and clearly.

- Example for **topic A:** *My favourite animals are lions and tigers. They are very big. They are very fast. They eat meat. I don't like giraffes. Giraffes are boring.*

- Example for **topic B:** *I live in a big house. I live with my mum, dad, sister and grandma. My favourite room is my bedroom. I have got a big bed and a desk. I do my homework in my bedroom.*

- Example for **topic C:** *I like rice. I eat rice every day. My mum can cook very well. Her cakes are delicious. I like rice with chicken and vegetables. I also like ice-cream.*

- Example for **topic D:** *I have many hobbies. I play football every weekend with my friends. I can play the guitar. I like swimming, but I can't swim very well. I want to do karate. I don't like reading.*

1. Match the sentence halves (1–6) and (A–F).

1. My favourite food
2. I love
3. My favourite
4. I like parrots
5. My favourite colours are
6. I can swim very well,

A monkeys.
B and cats.
C red and green.
D it's my favourite sport.
E is ice-cream.
F room is my bedroom.

2. Write each phrase from Exercise 1 in the correct topic box.

A HOUSES	B FOOD	C PETS
My favourite room is my bedroom.	_____ _____	_____ _____

D HOBBIES	E ANIMALS	F COLOURS
_____ _____	_____ _____	_____ _____

3. Look at these topic cards. Work with a partner. Talk for one minute about each topic. Use the sentences from Exercise 1 to help you.

A	B	C	D
My favourite animals	My house	My favourite food	My hobbies

4. Add two topic boxes. Write two sentences for each topic.

1. _____
2. _____

1. _____
2. _____

Activities for *Springboard* Task 1

The *Listening* exercises can be difficult. Ask your teacher or parent to help you.

Remember:

- Read the instructions carefully.
- Listen to the audio twice.
- Listen for information you need to complete the exercise.
- Check your answers.

TOP TIPS

First, look at the pictures.

- Who is in the picture?
- How do they look?
- What are they doing?

Do Exercises 1, 2 and 3 on page 31.

Do you need to review the grammar?
Review

- the *present continuous*.

Think about this topic:

- *the time.*

☞ In Exercise 1, choose the correct picture (A or B).

In **recording** 🎧12 (page 45), you will hear three things that will help you.

Remember: you have to listen for specific details.

- Circle the things in the picture you hear in the audio (time, toy, kangaroo, ...)
- Olivia gives the welcome banner to Nick when she sees Tom.

☞ In Exercise 2, say what Tom's friends are doing.

In **recording** 🎧13 (page 46), you will hear information about four people.

Remember: you have to say what they are doing in the picture.

1. Julie is standing near the tree.
2. Barbara is running.
3. The other boy is called Dan.
4. Phil is catching the ball.

☞ In Exercise 3, say what Tom's friends are wearing.

In **recording** 🎧14 (page 46), you will hear the information.

Remember: look for similarities and differences between the pictures.

- There are two pirates. Dan is wearing a belt and a hat. Phil has a black patch on his eye and a parrot.
- Julie has a big snowman costume and a hat.
- Barbara is holding flowers and is dressed as a butterfly.

1. Listen to recording 🎧12 and look at the pictures. Tick picture A or B.

2. Listen to recording 🎧13 . What are Tom's friends doing? Match the pictures (A–D) to the sentences (1–4). Draw lines. Write the names.

1. He is hitting the ball.

2. He is catching the ball.

3. She is standing near the tree.

4. She is running.

3. Listen to recording 🎧14 . What are Tom's friends wearing? Match the pictures (A–D) to the names (1–4). Draw lines.

1. Dan

2. Phil

3. Julie

4. Barbara

Activities for *Springboard* Task 2

The *Listening* exercises can be difficult. Ask your teacher or parent to help you.

Remember:

- Read the instructions carefully.
- Listen to the audio twice.
- Listen for information you need to complete the exercise.
- Only one picture is correct.
- Check your answers.

TOP TIPS

First, look at the pictures.

- Who or what do you see in the picture?
- Are they people or things?
- What are they doing?
- What else do you see?

Do Exercises 1, 2 and 3 on page 33.

Do you need to review the grammar?

Review

- the verb *have / has got* and the verb *can*.

Think about these topics:

- *houses*
- *seasons and weather*.

☞ In Exercise 1, choose the correct picture (A or B).

In **recording** 🎧15 (page 46), you will hear four things.

Remember: you have to listen carefully to the details.

- Tick the picture that Tom describes with affirmative sentences (*Yes, we have ...*).
- Cross out the picture that Tom describes with negative sentences (*No, we don't have ...*)

☞ In Exercise 2, choose the correct picture (A or B).

In **recording** 🎧16 (page 46), you will hear the information.

Remember: only one answer is correct.

☞ In Exercise 3, choose the correct picture (A, B or C).

In **recording** 🎧17 (page 46), you will hear the information.

Remember: only one answer is correct.

- See the key words highlighted on page 46.

1. Listen to recording 🎧15 and look at the pictures. Tick picture A or B.

A ☐

B ☐

2. Now listen to recording 🎧16 and look at the pictures. Read the questions (1–3) and tick picture A or B.

1. What does Nick need help with?

A ☐

B ☐

2. Who loves Maths?

A ☐

B ☐

3. What does Mrs Turner teach?

A ☐

B ☐

3. Listen to recording 🎧17 and look at the pictures. Read the questions (1–3) and tick picture A, B or C.

1. When does Olivia want Tom to come back?

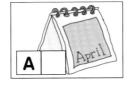
A ☐

B ☐

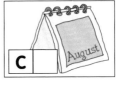
C ☐

2. Where does Tom go to celebrate in December?

A ☐

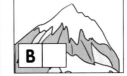
B ☐

C ☐

3. Does Olivia want to go to Australia in December?

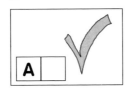
A ☐

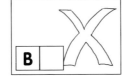
B ☐

C ☐

Activities for *Springboard* Task 3

It helps to know lots of words and grammar points to do these *Reading* and *Writing* exercises. Ask your teacher or parent to help you.

Remember:

- Read the instructions carefully.
- Think about the words you need.
- Check your answers.

TOP TIPS

First, read the answers.

- What does the dialogue talk about?
- What kind of questions are they?

If the answer is *Yes* or *No*, the question is a **closed question** (for example, *Have you got a pen?*, *Are you happy?*, *Can she swim?*).

If the answer gives more information or an opinion, the question is an **open question** (for example: *How old is your Dad?*, *Where do you live?*).

In English, questions starting with *Wh-* are always open questions. The answer to a *Wh-* question is never *Yes* or *No*.

Do Exercises 1, 2 and 3 on page 35.

Do you need to review the grammar?

Review

- words to ask questions (*What, Where, Who, ...*)
- word order in sentences
- frequency adverbs (*often, always, sometimes, ...*).

Think about these topics:

- *free time*
- *hobbies.*

☞ In Exercise 1, complete the questions with words from the box.

Remember: check if you need one question word (*When..., What...*) or an auxiliary verb (*Do ..., Have ..., Can ...*).

If you need *Do ..., Have ..., Can ...* to complete the question, check the answer: it is usually repeated in the answer! For example, *Can you ...? Yes, I can.*

☞ In Exercise 2, complete the beginning of the questions.

Remember:

- look at the answers first.

- we use *How often ...* to ask how many times an action is performed.
- we use *How long ...* to ask how much time something goes on.

☞ In Exercise 3, complete the end of the questions.

Remember:

- look at the answers first.
- underline the key information in the answer.
- use the key information to think about the question.

1. Write one question word from the box below in each space in the questions (1–5).

> Is · Do · When · What · Have

1. _____ is summer in Australia?
Summer in Australia is in December, January and February.

2. _____ it cold in summer?
No, it is very hot.

3. _____ sports do you play in the summer?
I go swimming.

4. _____ you got a summer uniform at school?
Yes, we have. We wear long, grey shorts and a red T-shirt.

5. _____ you get very hot outside at school?
No, we don't. We wear suncream and baseball hats.

Nick asks Tom to tell him about a typical Australian summer.

2. Complete these questions (1–5).

1. _____ do you go to the beach?
Every day. I love going to the beach in the summer.

2. _____ you swim very well in the sea?
Yes, I can. I'm a strong swimmer.

3. _____ you like surfing?
No, I don't. I prefer sailing.

4. _____ you got a boat?
No, I haven't, but my best friend, John, has got a canoe.

5. _____ does the film last?
It's on from 7.30 p.m. to 9.30 p.m. So, two hours.

3. Complete these questions (1–5).

1. Do _____ ?
No, I don't live near the beach. I live in the country.

2. Who _____ ?
Michael is my best friend.

3. How _____ ?
I go to school by bike.

4. Do _____ ?
Yes, we play football every weekend.

5. Can _____ ?
Yes, I can play basketball. I've got lots of trophies in my bedroom.

Activities for *Springboard* Task 4

It helps to know lots of words and grammar points to do these *Reading* and *Writing* exercises. Ask your teacher or parent to help you.

Remember:

- Read the instructions carefully.
- Look for words that describe objects or actions you see in the pictures.
- There are two extra sentences.
- Check your answers.

TOP TIPS

First, look at the pictures.

- What do you see in the picture?
- Who do you see?
- What is happening?
- Pay attention to the details.

Do Exercises 1 and 2 on page 37.

Do you need to review the grammar?

Review

- the verb *can* for requests and abilities
- the *present continuous*
- prepositions of place (*under, over, ...*).

Think about this topic:

- *clothes.*

☞ In Exercise 1, choose the correct picture (A or B) for each sentence.

Remember: read what people say, and choose the picture that matches it.

- Sentence 1 – Dad is asking for tickets.
- Sentence 2 – Dad wants to buy tickets for everyone (two adults and three children).
- Sentence 3 – The man says welcome to the show.
- Sentence 4 – Dad buys popcorn for the children.
- Sentence 5 – The show is about to begin, not to end.

☞ In Exercise 2, match each picture to the correct sentence.

Remember: you have to choose the sentence that matches what you see in the picture.

- Look at what's happening. Pay attention to the details.
- Read sentences 4 and 6 carefully. Then sentences 3 and 5!

1. Read the sentences (1–5). Tick picture A or B for each sentence.

1. Good evening. Can I have five tickets, please?

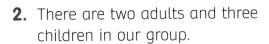

2. There are two adults and three children in our group.

3. Come in. Welcome to the show.

4. Do you want some popcorn?

5. Quiet, the show is starting!

2. Read the sentences (1–7). Match each sentence (1–7) to the correct picture (A–E). Be careful. There are two extra sentences.

1. Wow! Look! He's so high up.

2. Can I have one of those balloons, Mum?

3. Mum, look! He's jumping over the circle! What a great show!

4. Listen to the guitar player! She's very good!

5. Mum, look! He's so strong! What a great show!

6. Listen to the guitar player! He's very good!

7. The juggler is very good! He can throw six balls at the same time.

Activities for *Springboard* Task 5

It helps to know lots of words and grammar points to do these *Reading* and *Writing* exercises. Ask your teacher or parent to help you.

Remember:

- Read the instructions carefully.
- Think about what kind of words you need for each space (verb, noun, adjective, ...).
- There are some extra words.
- Check your answers.

TOP TIPS

First, read the text and the words in the box.

- What is the text about?
- Which words in the box can you use to complete the sentences?
- Do you need a noun, a verb, an adjective, a pronoun, ...?
- Which words in the box do you need?

Do Exercises 1, 2 and 3 on page 39.

Do you need to review the grammar?

Review

- prepositions (*to, on, at, in, ...*)
- the verb *to be*
- frequency adverbs (*often, always, sometimes, ...*).

Think about these topics:

- *school*
- *sports.*

☞ In Exercise 2, choose the correct words.

Remember: only one of the words is correct.

- *On* is used before the days of the week (*on Monday*) and to say where a thing is (*on the table*).
- *At* is used before the hour (*at 7 p.m*) and for a place where people are (*at the park*).
- *A* becomes *an* before a word that starts with a vowel (*an elephant*).

Remember: the letter *h* is a consonant!

☞ In Exercise 3, write the missing words.

Remember: you have to look for a word that matches the context of the sentence and is grammatically correct.

- What is Tom talking about?
- What are the words before and after the space?
- What kind of word is missing? Is it a word for a day, an hour, a place? Is it a verb?
- What words do you need to complete the sentence?

1. Tom is back home in Australia. Nick wants to send him an email.

Look at the phrases in the box. Write each phrase from the email in the correct column.

> Write soon. • Hi Tom! • How are you?
> We've got a new teacher. • Love, Nick
> Are you back at school?

START	MIDDLE	END
_____	_____	_____
_____	_____	_____

2. Now help Nick to finish his email to Tom. Underline the correct words.

Hi Tom!
How are you? I'm back (1) **on/at** school now.
We've got (2) **a/an** new teacher. Her name is Mrs Gonzalez. (3)
He's/She's Spanish.
Her lessons are great, but we get a lot of homework.
(4) **Are/Is** you back at school?
I've got a football match now, sorry!
Write (5) **quick/soon**.

Love,
Nick

3. Tom wants to reply to Nick. Help him to finish his email. Use the words in the box. Be careful, there are some extra words.

> from • school • your • can
> any • some • at

Dear Nick,
Thanks for (1) _____ email!
I'm back at (2) _____ too.
We haven't got (3) _____ new teachers and my English lessons
are still boring!
We have got a new football teacher. He's called Mr Pinket.
He's (4) _____ London. He's fantastic and we (5) _____ all play
much better now.

Write soon!
Tom

Activities for *Springboard* Task 6

It helps to know many words and grammar points to do these *Writing* exercises. Ask your teacher or parent to help you.
Remember:

- Read the instructions carefully.
- Think about the information you need.
- Check your answers.

TOP TIPS

First, read the questions.

- What are the questions about?
- Which words do you know about this topic?

Do Exercises 1, 2 and 3 on page 41.

Do you need to review the grammar?
Review

- words to ask questions (*What, Where, Who, ...*)
- the *present continuous*
- frequency adverbs (*often, always, sometimes, ...*).

Think about this topic:

- *holidays.*

☞ In Exercise 1, write six words about holidays.

Remember: there are no right or wrong answers. Write words you remember well and can spell correctly.

- Examples for holidays: *mountains, sea, beach, boat, ice-cream, playing, walking, ...*

☞ In Exercise 3, answer the questions.

Remember: you have to write about 30 words, but do not take too much time counting them. That's about six words for each answer. It's not much!

Examples:

1. *How often do you go on holiday?* Once a year, in the summer.
2. *Where do you usually go on your holidays?* To the beaches in the South.
3. *Where do you usually stay?* In a house, near the beach.
4. *Do you like reading on your holidays?* No, I don't. I prefer swimming.
5. *What kind of clothes do you take on holiday?* Sunglasses, T-shirts, a hat and flip-flops.

1. Complete this mind map. Write six words connected to holidays.

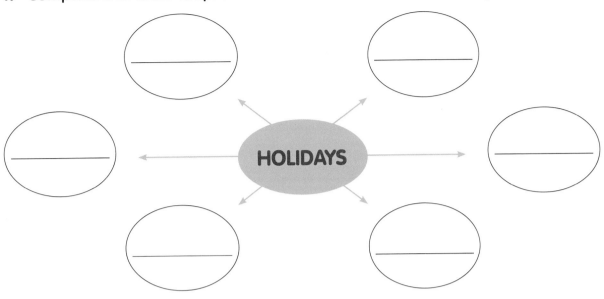

2. Look at the table. Tick the correct answers for YOU.

Where do you go on holiday?	☐ the mountains	☐ the seaside	☐ a city
Who do you go on holiday with?	☐ my family	☐ my grandparents	☐ my friends
What do you do on holiday?	☐ play	☐ study	☐ explore
Where do you sleep on holiday?	☐ in a hotel	☐ in a house	☐ in a tent
How do you get to your holiday destination?	☐ by plane	☐ by train	☐ by car

3. Answer the questions (1–5) about your holidays.

1. How often do you go on holiday? _____

2. Where do you usually go on your holidays? _____

3. Where do you usually stay? _____

4. Do you like reading on your holidays? _____

5. What kind of clothes do you take on holiday? _____

Activities for *Springboard Speaking* Tasks 7 and 8

The *Speaking* exercises can be difficult. Ask your teacher or parent to help you

Remember:

- Listen to the examiner's instructions.
- Always ask and answer questions in sentences.
- Show the examiner that you know the grammar and vocabulary.
- Ask the examiner if you do not understand something.

TOP TIPS

First, look at the pictures and read the cards.

- What do you see in the picture?
- Can you pronounce the question on the card?
- Can you answer the question?
- Look at the topic on the topic card. Think about the words you remember about the topic.

Remember: count out loud in English as you move from square to square on the board game!

Do Exercises 1, 2 and 3 on page 43.

Do you need to review the grammar?

See the list on page 9. What topics do you need to study?

☞ In Exercise 1, **ask and answer questions.**

Remember: use *What* to ask names, *How old* for ages, *Where* for places and *Can* for skills.

☞ In Exercise 2, **answer the questions.**

A   *How often do you go to the cinema?*

B   *How many hours of TV do you watch every week?*

C   *How do you get to school?*

D   *How much homework do you do every day?*

Remember: we use *How often* for questions about how many times you do something, and *How* to ask what you use to do something.

☞ In Exercise 3, **talk about these topics.**

A   *My favourite day*

B   *Dinner in my house*

C   *Places to go in my town*

D   *The summer holidays*

Remember: you have to speak for one minute. Do not go too fast: speak slowly and clearly.

- Example for **topic A:** *My favourite day is Monday. I like Mondays because I play basketball.*

- Example for **topic B:** *In my house, we have dinner at 7 p.m.*

- Example for **topic C:** *My town is very big. There are a lot of things to do.*

- Example for **topic D:** *I go to the mountains every summer for my holidays. It is nice and cool.*

1. Read Mr Green's profile for his company web page. Work with a partner. Take it in turns to ask and answer questions about Mr Green.

Name: Robert Green
Age: 46
Address: 10 King Street, York
Job Title: IT programmer
Other skills: Speaks French

2. Look at these squares from a board game. Work with a partner. Ask and answer the questions.

How often do you go to the cinema?

How many hours of TV do you watch every week?

How do you get to school?

How much homework do you do every day?

3. Look at these topic cards. Work with a partner. Talk for one minute about each topic.

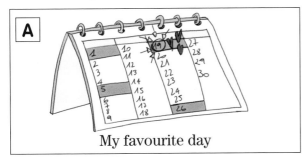

My favourite day

Dinner in my house

Places to go in my town

The summer holidays

Audio scripts

Recording 2 (pages 10–11)

Mum: Hi, Olivia! Do you want to come to the supermarket?

Olivia: No, thanks, Mum.

Mum: I don't want you to play games on your tablet all day.

Olivia: I'm not playing games, Mum. I'm sending an email to Samantha.

Recording 3 (pages 10–11)

Mum: Olivia?

Olivia: What, Mum?

Mum: Come outside, it's a beautiful day.

Olivia: I don't want to, Mum. I'm comfortable on the sofa in the living room.

Mum: OK then, but lunch is in the garden in ten minutes. Get some glasses from the kitchen, please.

Recording 4 (pages 12–13)

Nick: Where do you want to go on our day out, Olivia?

Olivia: Hmm ... I want to go to the cinema.

Nick: Boring! Let's go to the park.

Olivia: The park?

Nick: Yes, the park. Then I can play football with my friends.

Olivia: No, that is boring! I prefer to stay at home!

Recording 5 (pages 12–13)

Mum: So, where do you want to go on our day out?

Nick: The park!

Olivia: No, the cinema!

Mum: Come on, let's go somewhere everybody likes.

Olivia: I know, the museum!

Nick: Yeah!

Mum: OK, when do you want to go? Today?

Nick: No, let's go tomorrow.

Olivia: Yes. Grandma and Grandad can come too.

Nick: Yes!

Hamish the dog: WOOF WOOF!

Olivia: Sorry, Hamish, you can't come to the museum with us.

Mum: And me?

Nick: Yes, Mum. We want you and Dad to come too!

Recording 6 (pages 14–15)

Olivia: Dad, where's Nick?

Dad: He's over there.

Olivia: Is he with Tom?

Dad: I don't know. He's talking to a short, thin boy.

Olivia: No, Dad. Tom isn't short and thin. Tom is tall and thin. Has the boy got short, brown hair?

Dad: Yes, I think ...

Olivia: Ah! OK ...

Dad: Look... there – he's with Mike.

Olivia: Dad! That isn't Mike. Mike is tall and thin, and he's got short, dark hair.

Dad: Hmm, tall ... thin ... with short, dark hair ... isn't that Justin?

Olivia: No, Dad, that's not Justin. Justin is short, but he has got glasses. That's Phil.

Dad: Hmmm... maybe I need glasses!

Recording 7 (pages 14–15)

Olivia: Hi, Phil! Where's Nick?

Phil: Hi, Olivia. He's with Justin. He can't find his glasses.

Olivia: Poor Justin!

Phil: Do you want to play basketball?

Olivia: No, thanks! I'm too short for basketball.

Phil: Mike and Justin are short, but they can play really well.

Olivia: I know, but I want to be tall like Tom, and I want short hair like you, Phil!

Recording 🎧8 (pages 16–17)

Nick: Look, Mum. There's Olivia. She's practising with another girl.

Mum: Where? There are a lot of girls on the stage.

Nick: Over there, next to the girl with the flowers in her hair.

Mum: There are two girls with flowers in their hair.

Nick: Ah yeah... not the girl in the T-shirt and black trousers. Olivia is next to the girl in the long dress.

Mum: Oh yes, there she is. Hello, Olivia!

Nick: Mum, be quiet!

Recording 🎧9 (pages 16–17)

Nick: The show is starting.

Dad: Great! Where's Olivia?

Nick: She's over there, behind her friend Viola.

Mum: Look, Viola is wearing flowers in her hair.

Dad: Is she wearing a skirt?

Nick: No, Dad, that's Asia. She lives on our street!

Dad: Ah yes. Does that boy in the hat and shorts live on our street?

Mum: No, that's Martin. He's in Olivia's class at school.

Nick: That girl is in Olivia's class too.

Mum: Who?

Nick: She's called Linda. She's got a teddy bear.

Mum: Ah yes, Linda! Has Linda got a sister?

Nick: Yes, she's in my class. She's called Annabelle. She's over there.

Mum: Has she got long hair?

Nick: No, she's got short hair. She's wearing trousers and a T-shirt.

Dad: Look, there's Sophie!

Nick: Who's Sophie?

Dad: Your cousin!

Nick: Oh yeah! Her hair is short now and she's wearing a long dress! Sophie never wears dresses.

Recording 🎧10 (pages 18–19)

Olivia: Nick, do you know when Grandma's birthday is?

Nick: I think it's this week, but I'm not sure

Olivia: Mum! When is Grandma's birthday?

Mum: It's next week.

Olivia: OK. Can I make her a cake?

Mum: Yes, cakes are her favourite food.

Olivia: I'll make a chocolate cake.

Mum: Are you going to buy Grandma a present?

Olivia: No, Nick is going to do that.

Recording 🎧11 (pages 18–19)

Nick: Mum, can we have a birthday party for Grandma next week?

Mum: Yes, that would be good, Nick.

Nick: Can we have the party at the swimming pool?

Mum: No, Nick! Grandma doesn't like swimming.

Nick: OK... can we have the party at the cinema?

Mum: No, Nick! Grandma doesn't like watching films.

Nick: I know... can we have the party at the park?

Mum: Oh yes. Grandma loves going to the park to see the ducks.

Nick: We can give the ducks some birthday cake!

Recording 🎧12 (pages 30–31)

Olivia: What time is it, Nick?

Nick: It's 6 o'clock. Why?

Olivia: Tom's plane lands in ten minutes.

Nick: Look, there he is!

Olivia: Where?

Nick: Over there. He's holding a toy kangaroo.

Olivia: Hey, Tom! Hold the welcome banner, Nick.

Recording (13) (pages 30–31)

Tom: This is my favourite photo. It's me and all my friends from the cricket team.

Nick: I love cricket!

Tom: Me too, but I'm not very good. My best friend Phil is very good.

Nick: Who is Phil?

Tom: He's catching the ball.

Nick: What's the name of the other boy?

Tom: That's Dan. He is hitting the ball.

Nick: Are there any girls on your team?

Tom: Yes, Julie and Barbara. Julie is standing near the tree in this photo.

Nick: What's Barbara doing in the photo?

Tom: She's running! There is a bee behind her head! She's very scared of bees.

Recording (14) (pages 30–31)

Tom: This is a photo of my birthday party. Everyone is wearing a costume.

Olivia: I love the costumes! Who's the girl with the big, white costume and the hat?

Nick: That's Julie. She's a snowman!

Nick: Who's that wearing a belt?

Tom: That's Dan. He's a pirate. Look, he's got a hat too.

Olivia: I love pirate costumes! Who's the other pirate, with the black patch on his eye?

Tom: That's Phil.

Nick: He's got a parrot too!

Olivia: Is the girl holding the flowers Barbara?

Tom: That's right. She's a butterfly.

Nick: Where are you, Tom? Are you wearing a costume?

Olivia: Yes, where are you, Tom? I can't see you!

Tom: I'm the invisible man!

Recording (15) (pages 32–33)

Tom: Come and visit me with Nick next summer. Our house is really big!

Olivia: Have you got a swimming pool?

Tom: Yes, we have and we've got a big garden too.

Olivia: Have you got tennis courts too, and a football pitch?

Tom: No, Olivia, we haven't. We live in a house, we don't live in a sports club!

Recording (16) (pages 32–33)

Nick: Tom, can you help me with my Maths homework, please?

Tom: Sure. I love Maths.

Nick: Really? I don't like Maths and I'm not very good at algebra.

Tom: My Maths teacher, Mr Leaning, is fantastic. His lessons are fun.

Nick: Fun? Our Maths lessons are always boring. School in Australia sounds great!

Tom: No! We have boring lessons too. The boring lessons at my school are the English lessons. We always fall asleep!

Nick: English is my favourite subject. Mrs Turner is really cool.

Recording (17) (pages 32–33)

Olivia: Tom, can you come and visit again in December?

Tom: No, sorry, Olivia. I love December in Australia. We go to the beach.

Olivia: You can't go to the beach in December! The beach is for summer holidays.

Tom: It is summer in December in Australia!

Olivia: Oh yeah... Do you have snow?

Tom: No, we don't have snow, Olivia.

Olivia: That's terrible. December in Australia with the sunshine and no snow? No, thank you!

Past Papers

Firstwords

Springboard

Firstwords **Written test**

Leave blank

Hello kids, hello boys and girls. Today's test is Firstwords. Tasks One and Two are listening. Good luck and have fun!!

1. **Task One: A New Swimming Pool (16 marks)**

   Ben is calling home on his mobile phone. Listen to the conversation. After each part of the conversation, answer the question. Put a cross (☒) in the box under the correct picture.

   You will hear the conversation twice. First, listen to the example.

   Example: Who is Ben speaking to?

   A ☐   B ☒   C ☐

1. Who is Ben with?

   A ☐   B ☐   C ☐

2. Where is Ben?

   A ☐   B ☐   C ☐

3. What is Zoe doing?

A  ☐   B  ☒   C ☐

4. Where is the new swimming pool?

A  ☐   B  ☐   C ☐

5. Where is the small pool?

A  ☐   B  ☐   C ☐

6. How many children are there in the small pool?

2   4   6

A ☐   B ☐   C ☐

7. What is Ben's favourite food?

A ☐   B ☐   C ☐

8. How much money has Ben got with him?

A ☐   B ☐   C ☐

Task 1

(Total 16 marks)

Leave
blank

2. **Task Two: The Browns at the New Swimming Pool (14 marks)**

The next week, the Brown family go to the new swimming pool. Ben sees some of his friends there. Listen to the conversation. After each part of the conversation, draw a line from the name of the person to the correct picture.

Be careful. There are two extra pictures.

You will hear the conversation twice. First, listen to the example.

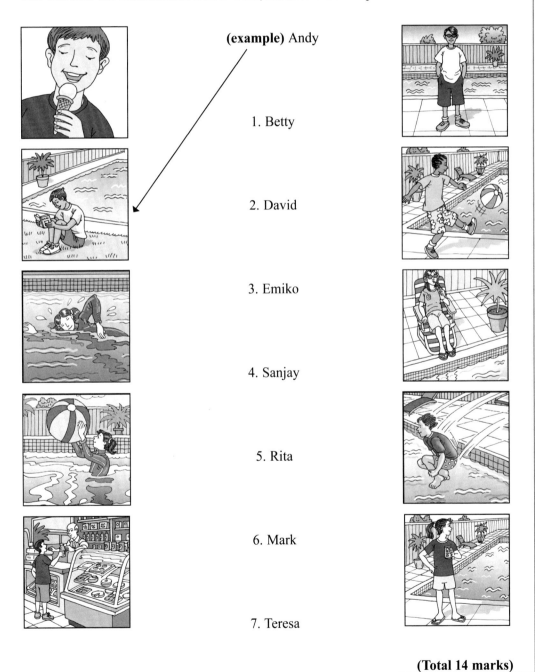

(example) Andy

1. Betty

2. David

3. Emiko

4. Sanjay

5. Rita

6. Mark

7. Teresa

Task 2

(Total 14 marks)

THAT IS THE END OF THE LISTENING TASKS. NOW GO ON TO TASK THREE.

3.   **Task Three: Sophie Talks to Teresa (10 marks)**

At the swimming pool, Sophie asks Teresa some questions. Draw a line from Sophie's questions to Teresa's answers. The first one is an example.

Be careful. There is one extra answer.

Example: Do you like the new swimming pool?

My mum and my brother Kevin.

1.   Are you a good swimmer?

He's in the pool with friends.

2.   Who are you here with?

~~Yes, its great.~~

Kevin is a good swimmer.

3.   Where is your mum?

Yes, let's go to the café.

4.   And what is Kevin doing?

Not very good but I can swim.

She's buying some drinks at the café.

5.   Do you want a drink?

(Total 10 marks)

4. **Task Four: At the Pool (10 marks)**

Look at the pictures of the Brown family at the new swimming pool and draw a line from the pictures to the correct sentences. The first one is an example.

Be careful. There is one extra sentence.

Can I have one of those please?

Try and catch this!

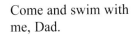

~~How much is a family ticket?~~

What are you doing with that ball?

Come and swim with me, Dad.

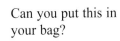

Can you put this in your bag?

I'm tired. Let's get out.

(Total 10 marks)

Task 4

5. **Task Five: Things at the Swimming Pool (16 marks)**

The Brown family see many things at the swimming pool. Draw a line from the pictures of the things to the words. The first one is an example.

Be careful. There are two extra words.

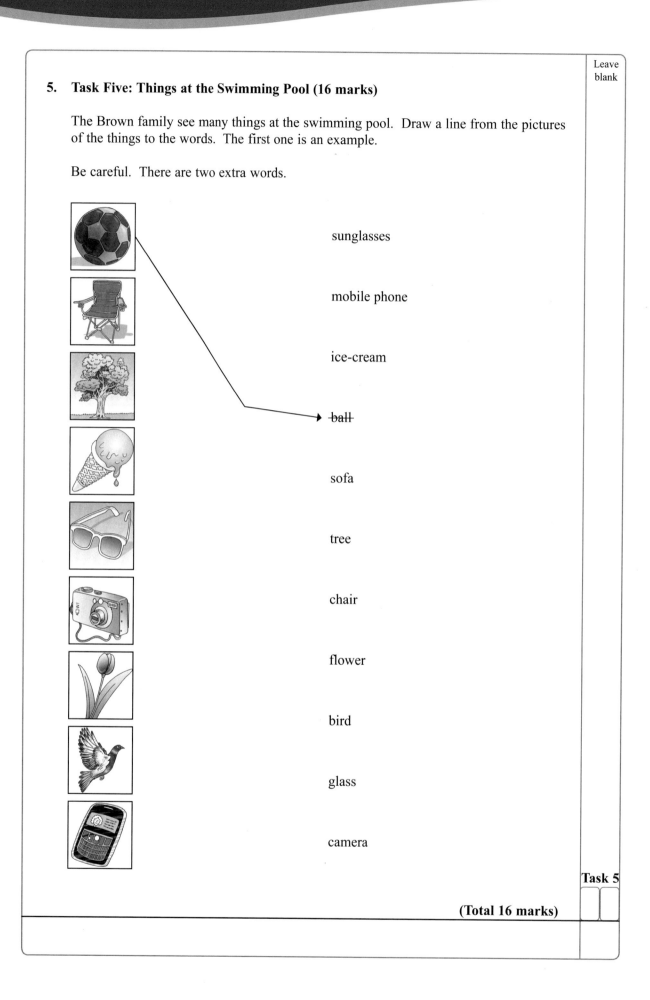

sunglasses

mobile phone

ice-cream

ball

sofa

tree

chair

flower

bird

glass

camera

Task 5

(Total 16 marks)

6. **Task Six: Our New Swimming Pool (14 marks)**

Ben writes in his diary about the new swimming pool. Help him to finish and write the missing words. Use the words in the box at the bottom of the page. Be careful. You do not need all of them. The first answer is an example.

There is a **(example)** ....**new**................... swimming pool in our

(1) .... It's big. There is a **(2)** ....

pool too but it is just for young **(3)** .... I like the new

swimming pool **(4)** .... much. It is fantastic. I have got a lot

of **(5)** .... I can meet them at the swimming pool and we can

(6) .... and play together. There is a **(7)** ....

there too

very	boy	children	swim	small
café	friends	~~new~~	football	old	town

Task 6

(Total 14 marks)

TOTAL FOR PAPER: 80 MARKS

THAT IS THE END OF THE TEST

Firstwords Spoken test

Instructions for the Oral Examiner

Before conducting the oral test the oral examiner must read the guidance notes inside the current version of the booklet "PTE Young Learners Oral Examination Guide". This booklet will be sent to the test centre by email, three weeks before the date of the written examination. If you have any queries, please contact Language Testing Division of Pearson by emailing pltsupport@pearson.com.

Oral Test

The oral test is a compulsory part of the Pearson Test of English Young Learners. Candidates are examined in groups of five by a trained oral examiner who acts as both interviewer and assessor. At each level the oral test lasts 20 minutes and consists of two 10-minute tasks which focus on the language of the level being tested. The oral accounts for 20 marks.

Stages of the Exam

- The candidates do the board game.
- The candidates take turns picking a card from the pack of topic cards and talking about the topic written on it. After each mini-presentation the other candidates and, if needed, the examiner asks the speaker some questions about the topic.

Task 1: The Board Game

- Required: the board game itself (please cut out the squares from the card provided), dice, five coloured counters.

- Lay out the cards in a circle, a line or S-shape.

- Establish the order of turn taking. (E.g. each candidate rolls the dice and the highest scorer goes first).

- The first candidate rolls the dice and moves the appropriate number of squares. The examiner directs the candidate to address the question to another candidate, referred to by name (e.g. "Ask Fatima"). The candidate then reads out the question and the designated candidate answers it. The square is then turned face down to remove it from the game. The turn passes to the next candidate.

- When moving their counters, candidates should count the squares **in English**.

- Each candidate should respond to at least two questions.

The test is over when each candidate has responded to at least two questions. The game should last no longer than 10 minutes for a group of five candidates.

Task 2: Short Talks

The pack of topic cards is placed face down in the middle of the playing area. The first candidate turns over a card and reads the topic written on it. He or she then speaks about that topic for one minute. At the end of one minute the examiner asks the candidate to stop and invites the other candidates to ask follow-up questions, which the first candidate answers. This continues for one minute (giving the candidate a total turn of two minutes' duration). If the other candidates cannot think of any questions, or if they dry up before the minute is up, the examiner should ask questions. The turn then passes to the next candidate.

Firstwords cards for board game

Can you spell your name?

E-D-W-A-R-D

What is your favourite toy?

Where are your toys?

How many televisions are there in your house?

How many friends have you got?

How many rooms are there in your house?

What have you got in your bedroom?

How many people are there in your family?

Where are your mum and dad now?

What colour is your school bag?

Where can you listen to music in your house?

How many brothers and sisters have you got?

What is your mum's favourite animal?

Where are your friends now?

What is your favourite hobby?

What lessons have you got today?

How many desks are there in your classroom?

Where can you play with your friends?

What colour are your shoes?	How many books are there in your school bag?

Firstwords topic cards

One of my friends

My bedroom

My toys

My favourite book

My favourite singer

My school

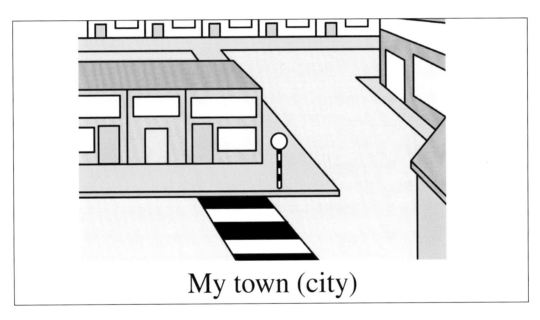

My town (city)

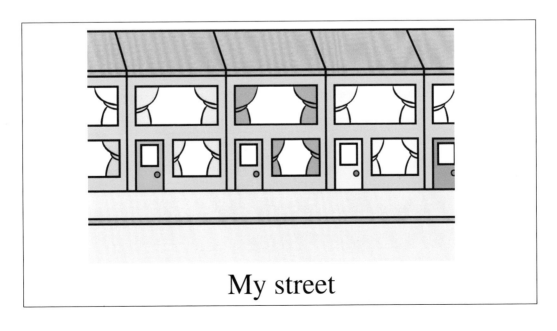

My street

My friend's pets

Food in the house

A big animal

My favourite food

My favourite toy

My favourite teacher

Springboard Written test

Leave blank

Hello kids, hello boys and girls. Today's test is Springboard. Tasks One and Two are listening. Good luck and have fun!!

1. **Task One: The New Art Gallery (16 marks)**

Mrs Brown and Ben are talking about a new art gallery. Listen to their conversation. After each part of the conversation, answer the question. Put a cross (⊠) in the box under the correct picture.

You will hear the conversation twice. First, listen to the example.

Example: Where is Ben?

A ☐   B ☐   C ⊠

1. Where is the new art gallery?

A ☐   B ⊠   C ☐

2. Which is the right map?

  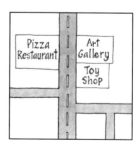

A ☐   B ☐   C ☐

3. What's in the toy shop window?

A ☐   B ☐   C ☐

4. What's the name of the art gallery?

A ☐   B ☐   C ☐

5. Which is the famous picture in Room One?

A ☐   B ☐   C ☐

6. How does Ben learn about art?

A ☐   B ☐   C ☐

7. What does Ben like painting now?

A  ☐   B  ☒   C ☐

8. What is Ben drawing for homework?

A  ☐   B  ☐   C ☐

Task 1

(Total 16 marks)

Leave blank

2. **Task Two: Which Pictures do They Like? (14 marks)**

Ben and Sophie are talking about the pictures in the new art gallery. Listen to their conversation. After each part of the conversation, draw a line from the name of the person to the correct picture.

Be careful. There are two extra pictures.

You will hear the conversation twice. First, listen to the example.

(example) Ben

1. Sophie

2. Laura

3. Heidi

4. Mrs White

5. Andy

6. Mr Moor

7. Jack

Task 2

(Total 14 marks)

THAT IS THE END OF THE LISTENING TASKS. NOW GO ON TO TASK THREE.

3. **Task Three: Ben Talks to Jane Clark (15 marks)**

Ben is in the art gallery. Jane Clark works in the gallery. Ben asks Jane about the gallery. What are Ben's questions? Write them in the spaces. The first one is an example.

Ben: **(example) _Do you like working here?_**

Jane: Yes, I love working here.

Ben: What .... ?

Jane: The gallery opens at nine o'clock.

Ben: Do .... ?

Jane: Not on Saturdays. But I do work on Sundays.

Ben: How many .... ?

Jane: There are six hundred pictures in the gallery.

Ben: Can .... ?

Jane: Yes. The gallery shop sells postcards.

Ben: Where .... ?

Jane: The Café? It's on the second floor.

Task 3

(Total 15 marks)

4. **Task Four: Drawing Pictures at Home (10 marks)**

Look at the people drawing pictures at home. Draw a line from the pictures to the correct sentences.

Be careful. There are two extra sentences.

The first one is an example.

Look! These two colours make purple.

This programme's giving me ideas for my homework.

~~Sit on that chair by the window.~~

They're moving too fast. I can't draw them.

No! Don't put it down there.

Thanks. I'm getting really hungry.

Here you are. Have a drink.

Hey. Come down! We want to draw you.

Task 4

(Total 10 marks)

5. Task Five: Sophie's Email to her Friend (15 marks)

Sophie is writing an email to her friend Neeta about her art homework. Help her to finish her email. Use the words in the box below. Be careful. You don't need all the words.

Hi Neeta,

How are you? What (**example**) .... *are* .... you doing today? I

(**1**) .... got some art homework. The homework is drawing one

of (**2**) .... rooms in our house. I am not very good at drawing

(**3**) .... I like it. I am in my own bedroom now and

(**4**) .... is really nice. In my bedroom (**5**) ....

is my bed, a desk and a big cupboard. Mum is making me some pink

(**6**) .... for the window. I (**7**) .... see the garden

from my window. I am drawing my bedroom (**8**) .... homework.

Our new cat, Poppy, is (**9**) .... on my bed with my teddy bears. She

is in my (**10**) .... too!

Write soon

Love Sophie

and	~~are~~	the	picture	can	curtains
for	have	asleep	but	it	there

(**Total 15 marks**)

6. **Task Six: Places in your Town (10 marks)**

Now write about places in your town.

1. Which is your favourite place to visit in your town?

    ....

2. What do you like doing there?

    ....

3. Who do you usually go there with?

    ....

4. Is there a museum or art gallery in your town?

    ....

5. What kinds of pictures do you like?

    ....   Task 6

                                                                    (Total 10 marks)

                                        TOTAL FOR PAPER: 80 MARKS

                        THAT IS THE END OF THE TEST

Springboard Spoken test

Instructions for the Oral Examiner

Before conducting the oral test the oral examiner must read the guidance notes inside the current version of the booklet "PTE Young Learners Oral Examination Guide". This booklet will be sent to the test centre by email, three weeks before the date of the written examination. If you have any queries, please contact Language Testing Division of Pearson by emailing pltsupport@pearson.com.

Oral Test

The oral test is a compulsory part of the Pearson Test of English Young Learners. Candidates are examined in groups of five by a trained oral examiner who acts as both interviewer and assessor. At each level the oral test lasts 20 minutes and consists of two 10-minute tasks which focus on the language of the level being tested. The oral accounts for 20 marks.

Stages of the Exam

- The candidates do the board game.
- The candidates take turns picking a card from the pack of topic cards and talking about the topic written on it. After each mini-presentation the other candidates and, if needed, the examiner asks the speaker some questions about the topic.

Task 1: The Board Game

- Required: the board game itself (please cut out the squares from the card provided), dice, five coloured counters.

- Lay out the cards in a circle, a line or S-shape.

- Establish the order of turn taking. (E.g. each candidate rolls the dice and the highest scorer goes first).

- The first candidate rolls the dice and moves the appropriate number of squares. The examiner directs the candidate to address the question to another candidate, referred to by name (e.g. "Ask Fatima"). The candidate then reads out the question and the designated candidate answers it. The square is then turned face down to remove it from the game. The turn passes to the next candidate.

- When moving their counters, candidates should count the squares **in English**.

- Each candidate should respond to at least two questions.

The test is over when each candidate has responded to at least two questions. The game should last no longer than 10 minutes for a group of five candidates.

Task 2: Short Talks

The pack of topic cards is placed face down in the middle of the playing area. The first candidate turns over a card and reads the topic written on it. He or she then speaks about that topic for one minute. At the end of one minute the examiner asks the candidate to stop and invites the other candidates to ask follow-up questions, which the first candidate answers. This continues for one minute (giving the candidate a total turn of two minutes' duration). If the other candidates cannot think of any questions, or if they dry up before the minute is up, the examiner should ask questions. The turn then passes to the next candidate.

Springboard cards for board game

Who do you play with at school? 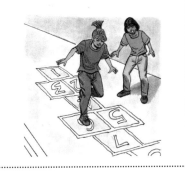	Where does your family eat dinner? 	Where do you do your homework? 
When do you go to the cinema? 	What do you usually have for breakfast? 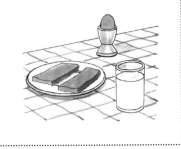	Can you play any instruments? 
How often do you eat in a restaurant? 	What do you do when you go to your friend's house? 	What is your favourite television programme? 

Who does the cooking in your house?

What sports can you play at school?

Who cleans your bedroom?

How many lessons a day do you have?

What is your favourite sport?

What clothes do you wear at school?

What time do you get up at the weekend?

How often do you play computer games?

How often do you go out with your parents?

When do your family have parties?

In your family, who can ride a bicycle?

Springboard topic cards

My family at the weekend

My breakfast, lunch and dinner

Winter in my country

My day at school

Things in my house

Summer in my country

Television in my house

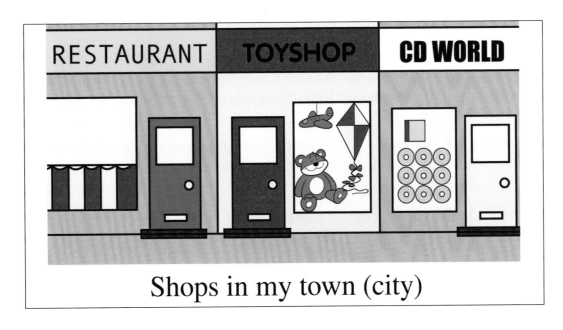

Shops in my town (city)

Cinemas in my town (city)

Sports in my town (city)

My favourite animal

My birthday

My homework

My friends and me

Pearson Education Limited
KAO Two
KAO Park
Hockham Way,
Harlow, Essex,
CM17 9SR England
and Associated Companies throughout the world.

www.english.com/teamtogether

First published 2020

ISBN: 978-1-292-29271-7

Set in Bauer Grotesk 12pt

Printed in Slovakia by Neografia

Illustrated by Luisa Cittone, Francesca Costa, Adam Linley, Robin Lawrie, Jim Eldridge and Mike Phillips

Cover image: *Front*: **Getty Images:** damircudic